An opinionated guide to

T0166793

# LONDON
# HOTELS

*Written by*
GINA JACKSON

Other opinionated guides:

*East London*

*London Architecture*

*Vegan London*

*London Green Spaces*

*Independent London*

*London Pubs*

*Sweet London*

*Kids' London*

*Escape London*

*Eco London*

*Big Kids' London*

*Art London*

*Free London*

*Queer London*

*London Delis*

# INFORMATION IS DEAD.
# LONG LIVE OPINION.

This book is useless. Everything you need to know about every hotel in London is available online. For free. Now. Generated by AI.

Except... that's exactly the problem, isn't it? It's all too much info. So with Gina's expert help, we've selected only the best. According to who? According to us!

Our usual refrain is that since we are locals publishing about our local area, these are the places we'd send you to if you came to stay on our couch. Although, in this instance, that doesn't hold, because we'd be suggesting you didn't stay on our couch, but rather in a hotel. Which would be rejecting you. Which we aren't. We welcome you. Just make sure to bring back some free toiletries, two croissants and a bathrobe.

Brown's (no.22)

*Inhabit Queen's Gardens (no.32)*

WISH YOU WERE HERE

TRIBE (no.9)

*Artist Residence (no.27)*

The Connaught (no.24)

# WE HOPE YOU ENJOY
# YOUR STAY

When booking a city break, it's natural to focus on all the amazing restaurants, bars, museums, shops and theatres that you'll visit, meaning that where to stay is often overlooked. But, for me, the hotel you choose can define your entire experience. There's no greater thrill than checking in and allowing yourself to be transported elsewhere, to a life where everyday worries float away in the time it takes to pour a luxurious bath and dial room service.

This is why I started reviewing hotels years ago on Instagram, authored a book about boutique hotels for Hoxton Mini Press, and now write about them as my full-time occupation (it's a hard job, but someone has to do it!).

Even as a Londoner (and I've lived here nearly all my life) there's nothing I love more than a staycation in my own city, basing myself in a new neighbourhood and pretending I'm a tourist so I can see London through fresh eyes. And there are plenty of ways to feel far from home without actually leaving: you can be nibbling on Cédric Grolet croissants (the best you'll find in London, so good you could almost be in Paris) on cloud-like banquettes at The Berkeley (no.34), or sipping a mezcal margarita at NoMad London's Side Hustle bar (no.1), reminiscent of a hip, upscale New York diner. London has it all, so why would you leave?

We've looked far and wide to curate the very best stays all over the city, whether you're looking for a design-led bolthole that's easier on the wallet or a five-star pad with all the frills, get a kick out of rubbing shoulders with A-listers in a former Victorian firehouse, or want to sleep where Tudor royals once rested their heads.

Of course, a sleepover in the capital is never going to be a bargain, but there are plenty of ways to experience the luxe London hotel lifestyle without forking out for an overnight stay. We've selected the best for you to sample, from a superb Sunday roast in the beautiful blue-panelled restaurant at The Twenty Two (no.18) to spritzers on the riverside terrace of The Mitre Hampton Court (no.17) and afternoon tea with a Japanese twist at Nobu Portman Square (no.31).

Looking to push the boat out for a special celebration? We've collated ideas for that too, whether your tastes lean towards a pampering massage and steam in the heavenly hammam at The Ned (no.5), or you prefer your indulgence in the form of Michelin-starred meals at The Connaught (no.24) and Town Hall Hotel (no.10). You might be surprised to discover that some of the city's best bars, restaurants and spas are hiding inside hotels that you've never heard of.

I hope this book encourages you to go out and experience everything that London has to offer, regardless of whether you're visiting from abroad, from elsewhere in Britain, or are based in the capital. I'm a firm believer that, often, the hotel very much *is* the destination… and after looking through this book, you might find that you agree.

Gina Jackson @*ginagoesto*
London, 2023

# BEST FOR...

### Afternoon tea

Visit the leafy Orangery at Soho favourite Ham Yard Hotel (no.26) for afternoon tea with a distinctly floral feel, or head to The Berkeley (no.34) for their legendary fashion-focused Prêt-à-Portea. For an Asian-inspired twist, Nobu Portman Square (no.31) offers a Japanese take on the classic tea, which includes scones with yuzu lemon curd and cream.

### Ultimate relaxation

For those in need of pampering, the spa at The Ned (no.5) offers everything from calming facials to LED light therapy in its Cowshed treatment rooms and generous pink marble hammam, while the Aman Spa at The Connaught (no.24) features a stunning water wall that cascades into the pool, and massages that will leave you feeling brand new.

### Celebration dinner

For gala nights out, gourmands can stay central for a feast with a view at tenth-floor restaurant Decimo at The Standard (no.6), or venture east to Da Terra at Town Hall Hotel (no.10). For a meal that's equally charming, the elegant interiors of Chiltern Firehouse (no.21) and NoMad London (no.1) bring the wow factor too.

### Cocktails with friends

For intimate gatherings, the secretive Punch Room at London EDITION (no.19) and The Malt Lounge at The Prince Akatoki (no.28) are two of London's best-kept secrets. Sample award-winning cocktails at the subterranean Seed Library at One Hundred Shoreditch (no.13), or put yourself in the hands of expert mixologists at Scarfes Bar at The Rosewood (no.8).

### Date night

Feeling the love? Treat your significant other to exceptional food and wine with an overnight stay at chic Beaverbrook Townhouse (no.33) or Mayfair favourite Brown's (no.22). Further afield, escape the hustle of central London for romance on the river at Bingham Riverhouse (no.36).

### Luxury on a budget

Want a design-led stay without the designer price tag? Luckily there are plenty of options, from the slick Bermonds Locke (no.16) to tranquil Inhabit Queen's Gardens (no.32) and trendy TRIBE in Canary Wharf (no.9). And any of the Hoxton hotels (no.2, no.15 and no.38) offer style without breaking the bank.

### No expense spared

If you're in the mood to push the boat out, The Berkeley (no.34) and Claridge's (no.20) are famous names that won't fail to deliver, with spacious suites, five-star service, and dizzying food and drink offerings. Meanwhile, rooms at The Cadogan, A Belmond Hotel (no.30) and The Twenty Two (no.18) are equally as elegant and fly slightly under the radar.

1

# NOMAD LONDON

*Old-world glamour in the West End*

Just off Covent Garden's piazza, NoMad London occupies what used to be the Bow Street Magistrates' Court and Police Station. But inside you'll find New York-style glamour with lots of theatricality – draped curtains, chintz and lacquered surfaces – and 1,600 artworks that were commissioned for the hotel. Bedrooms, several with views of the Royal Opera House, feature beautiful mosaic bathrooms and suites have in-room roll top tubs. The restaurant occupies a dramatic light-filled atrium with trailing greenery, where you can eat breakfast through to dinner (don't miss the lemon ricotta pancakes). Have a pre-theatre tipple at Side Hustle, the Latin American-inspired speakeasy, or Common Decency – the subterranean cocktail lounge named after the infamous Oscar Wilde trial that was held here.

*28 Bow Street, WC2E 7AW*
*Nearest station: Covent Garden*
*thenomadhotel.com/london*

2

# THE HOXTON, HOLBORN

*Contemporary cool in a prime location*

The lively lobby here is a great place to lounge on the squishy sofas and watch a steady stream of visitors pop by the open-plan coffee shop, bar and all-day restaurant Rondo. Upstairs, the bedrooms nod to the building's history as a former telephone exchange, with an industrial-luxe style, and range in size from 'shoebox' to 'biggy'. Retro Roberts radios are in every room, and breakfast bags outside your door each morning are a nice touch. Don't miss the thick Detroit-style pizza slices at intimate wine bar La Cave – one of London's best-kept secrets. And the icing on the cake? The flexible check-in and out policy, giving you more time to wander to the British Museum, shop Oxford Street or stroll around Covent Garden.

*199–206 High Holborn, WC1V 7BD*
*Nearest station: Holborn*
*thehoxton.com/london/holborn*

3

# HENRIETTA HOTEL

*French flair in theatreland*

This boutique townhouse hotel from French hospitality brand the Experimental Group (responsible for the Experimental Cocktail Club) has plenty of theatrical touches, as befits the surrounding area. Showstopping rooms feature sweeping curved headboards, gold lampshades and velvet armchairs, and the Instagram-worthy bathrooms are painted in the hotel's signature pale pink. A further 22 bedrooms can be found in a private townhouse across the street. In a neighbourhood like this, you'll never be far from revelry and are moments from the West End's best restaurants, bars and theatres. If you'd rather dine closer to home, Da Henrietta, the stylish Italian restaurant on the ground floor, offers a seasonal menu of sharing plates.

*14–15 Henrietta Street, WC2E 8PS*
*Nearest stations: Covent Garden, Leicester Square*
*henriettahotel.com*

4

# THE MONDRIAN

*Slick Shoreditch sleepover with a rooftop pool*

There's a lot to stimulate the senses at The Mondrian, reflecting the lively neighbourhood around it. Inside this sleek warehouse conversion, bedrooms featuring generous terraces bring the outside in with exposed brick and artwork that's reminiscent of the colourful graffiti on the streets below. Enjoy an aperitivo at the hotel's leafy cafe-come-cocktail bar Christina's before moving downstairs for dinner at BiBo, the subterranean Spanish restaurant by Michelin-starred chef Dani García. Bag a booth for delicious tapas, or head up to rooftop restaurant Laurel's, where you'll also find an outdoor pool and wraparound terrace. Hungry for more? There's a 24/7 gym, spa offering everything from seaweed wraps to candlelit CBD massages, plus a members' club and cinema.

*45 Curtain Road, EC2A 3PT*
*Nearest station: Shoreditch High Street*
*book.ennismore.com/hotels/mondrian/shoreditch*

5

# THE NED

*Old-school glamour in the square mile*

Occupying the gargantuan building that was once the Midland Bank HQ, this city slickers' playground hosts a private members' club and a rooftop pool and bar with views over the City and St Paul's Cathedral. You'll be serenaded with live music every evening, regardless of where you are dining – there are seven restaurants in what was once the cavernous banking lobby. 1920s glamour is maintained throughout the 250 bedrooms and suites, with mahogany panelling, four-posters and roll top tubs, while cosy comforts are supplied in the form of sumptuous robes and Cowshed toiletries. If you're lucky, the cocktail trolley may swing by before you head to dinner. Don't miss a visit to the underground spa for a pampering massage, or swim laps of the pool before steaming off in the pink marble hammam.

*27 Poultry, EC2R 8AJ*
*Nearest station: Bank*
*thened.com*

6

# THE STANDARD, LONDON

*Cool comfort and convenience*

King's Cross was aching for somewhere cool to stay before The Standard opened its doors in 2019. A Brutalist behemoth across from St Pancras International on Euston Road, the vibe here is bold and fun, with 266 bedrooms featuring 1970s colours and kitsch. The curved windows make it feel like you're peeping out of a submarine porthole, and some of the larger suites benefit from outdoor tubs on the terrace. Whizz up to the tenth-floor restaurant Decimo (using the bright red lift pod on the outside of the building, naturally), where sensational flavour-packed tortilla and croquetas are plated up by Michelin-starred chef Peter Sanchez-Iglesias, and soak in the incredible views over the city with a mezcal cocktail.

*10 Argyle Street, WC1H 8EG*
*Nearest station: King's Cross St Pancras*
*standardhotels.com/london*

7

# KIMPTON FITZROY

*Grande dame of Bloomsbury*

For a true slice of Bloomsbury history, you can't beat the Kimpton Fitzroy; its hallowed halls, which run over an entire block opposite leafy Russell Square, were once a favourite spot of the famous literary group. The tea-coloured terracotta building is adorned with life-size statues of British queens, and you'll feel wrapped in regal resplendence as you cross the original mosaic floors. Ascend a marble staircase to the bedrooms, the largest of which have freestanding tubs and heavily draped four-posters in creamy neutrals. British brasserie Galvin Bar and Grill was designed by Charles Fitzroy Doll – who designed the dining room on the *Titanic* – while the coffee shop Burr & Co is in the former townhouse of suffragette Emmeline Pankhurst. Be sure to raise a glass to glorious residents past in glitzy Fitz's bar.

*1–8 Russell Square, WC1B 5BE*
*Nearest station: Russell Square*
*kimptonfitzroylondon.com*

8

# THE ROSEWOOD

*High society on High Holborn*

The Rosewood commands intrigue, with passers-by curious about what lies behind its imposing iron gates. Designed in a flamboyant Belle Époque style, it could easily pass for a French chateau with terrazzo floors and a jaw-dropping seven-storey Pavonazzo marble staircase. Upstairs in the suites, beds are enormous, bathrooms luxurious and pillowcases are embroidered with each guest's initials. Savour hearty British fare in the handsome Holborn Dining Room, where the famous pie menu has such a cult following that the restaurant has a dedicated Pie Room and serves takeaway pastries from its Pie Hole, then head to Scarfes Bar for live music and cocktails. You may need to fit in a trip to the spa during your stay, to work off the previous night's indulgence at the impressive gym.

*252 High Holborn, WC1V 7EN*
*Nearest station: Holborn*
*rosewoodhotels.com/en/london*

9

# TRIBE

*Coolest corner of Canary Wharf*

TRIBE is a breath of fresh air blowing through what is otherwise a corporate concrete jungle. Inside it is sleek and boldly colourful, feeling fun but functional. Feels Like June, the all-day Cali-inspired restaurant, is a great place to curl up on curved velvet sofas around terrazzo tables and tuck into generous stacks of buttermilk pancakes or tacos. This is a hub for guests, locals and tourists, with cocktails being sipped under the art at all times of day and night. Bedrooms are bright, comfortable and unfussy with floor-to-ceiling windows, and there's an all-day grab-and-go stand serving homemade treats 24/7 in case you're looking for a midnight snack.

*15 Water Street, E14 9QG*
*Nearest station: Canary Wharf*
*tribehotels.com/en/united-kingdom/london-canary-wharf*

10

# TOWN HALL HOTEL

*Old meets new in timeless style*

Perhaps east London's favourite Edwardian relic, Town Hall Hotel may be situated on Bethnal Green's busy Cambridge Heath Road, but inside it's a palace of relaxed opulence. You might recognise parts of the hotel from a famous film or two, from the huge subterranean swimming pool to the original council chamber. You can easily get lost here in the warren of leather-clad hallways that lead to almost a hundred rooms and suites, ranging from the three-storeyed De Montfort suite, featuring plenty of period details, to mid-century studios and newer hideaways decorated in uplifting pastels. Spoil yourself with two-Michelin-star meals at South American-inspired Da Terra, or for lighter bites opt for small plates at Restaurant Elis followed by cocktails at Silk Weaver.

*8 Patriot Square, E2 9NF*
*Nearest stations: Bethnal Green, Cambridge Heath*
*townhallhotel.com*

11

# REDCHURCH TOWNHOUSE

*Chic and compact crash pad*

Squeezed between stylish boutiques in the heart of foodie Shoreditch, this hotel fits in so well with its neighbours that you might unknowingly stride right past it. Soho House's furthest venture east is small but perfectly formed, full of stylish mid-century furniture and comfy leather armchairs. All rooms include fluffy bathrobes and Cowshed toiletries, along with little touches to elevate your stay: homemade chocolate chip cookies, a pouch of essentials in case you forgot your toothbrush, and an in-room cocktail bar so you can pour your own G&T. For dinner, join the crowd at refined trattoria Cecconi's and try out the signature spaghetti lobster. Alternatively, plenty more of Shoreditch's best restaurants are on your doorstep.

*25–27 Whitby Street, E1 6JU*
*Nearest station: Shoreditch High Street*
*sohohouse.com/bedrooms/redchurch-townhouse*

12

# THE STRATFORD

*Stylish sky-high base with a destination restaurant*

A soaring glass shard cutting into the east London skyline, The Stratford towers over Queen Elizabeth Olympic Park. Here you're ideally placed to explore everything east London has to offer, while you can also be in King's Cross in minutes by high-speed rail. A spectacular triple-height lobby sets the stage for the industrial-chic feel of the rest of the hotel. Spacious bedrooms are simple and smart in subdued palettes, with curved armchairs and brass fixtures that reference the luxe lofts of Manhattan, and larger, long-stay apartments are available. Kitchen E20 serves modern British fare, but the uncontested jewel in The Stratford's crown is Allegra, the seventh-floor restaurant, for refined Mediterranean dining among curved grey banquettes and hanging lamps, with a glowing, golden hour terrace.

*Olympic Park, 20 International Way, E20 1FD*
*Nearest station: Stratford International*
*thestratford.com*

13

# ONE HUNDRED SHOREDITCH

*Low-key cool with a top-notch rooftop bar*

In prime position on the high street, this is the perfect base for exploring the restaurants, clubs and bars of Shoreditch. The lobby is a hotspot for laptop-tapping freelancers who make use of the mid-century style deep leather sofas, long wooden tables and strong coffee from onsite cafe Coffee Shop. When you've had enough of the buzz, the bedrooms offer a calming retreat, decorated in neutral tones with super-comfy sofas to lounge on, rattan furnishings and abstract art. Don't miss the hotel's rooftop terrace, all dusty pink marble and hanging plants, which offers one of the best views in Shoreditch for enjoying a sundowner.

*100 Shoreditch High Street, E1 6JQ*
*Nearest station: Shoreditch High Street*
*onehundredshoreditch.com*

14

# MAMA SHELTER

*Funky funland with a local flavour*

When Mama Shelter opened its doors in 2019 it breathed new life into a tired corner of Bethnal Green. Now a mainstay of bustling Hackney Road, locals gather in the restaurant-come-lobby at all times of day beneath a hand-painted ceiling that pays homage to the city. In the evening there's a lively buzz around the foosball table and DJ booth, or you can head down to the basement where there's more fun to be found in the boutique games arcade and karaoke rooms. The daring, clashing prints downstairs give way to more simply styled bedrooms, but you'll still find playful touches including the brand's signature cartoon masks. Wake up to a generous buffet breakfast, and pick up a souvenir of your stay from the cabinet of Mama merch.

*437 Hackney Road, E2 8PP*
*Nearest stations: Cambridge Heath, Bethnal Green*
*mamashelter.com/london-shoreditch/stay*

15

# THE HOXTON, SOUTHWARK

*Sumptuous south London pad*

The Hoxton's first foray south of the river is a sleek 14-storey colossus of brick and glass, moments from the South Bank and within easy walking distance of cultural and foodie hotspots like Tate Modern and Borough Market. Bedrooms are cool and contemporary with lavish touches: claret-coloured velvet paired with pistachio panelling and gold hardware. The lobby is the perfect place to kick back with a cocktail or a coffee, while all-day dining restaurant Albie hosts a rotation of pop-ups that consistently draw a crowd. Or flock to Seabird, the stunning rooftop restaurant with tropical potted palms and fresh seafood, and enjoy panoramic views of Southwark from the outdoor terrace.

*40 Blackfriars Road, SE1 8NY*
*Nearest station: Blackfriars*
*thehoxton.com/london/southwark*

16

# BERMONDS LOCKE

*Calm Californian aparthotel*

The busy streets around Tower Bridge might not instantly provoke feelings of relaxation, but Bermonds Locke is seeking to change that. Inspired by the colours of the Mojave Desert, this aparthotel offers roomy studios in soft, sunset-hued pastels, with natural textures such as rattan shades, woven rugs and linen bedding. Each apartment is a home away from home, fitted out with its own kitchen. In the lobby there are ample places to plug in your laptop, and guests and freelancers spill out across the swing chairs and hip concrete tables by the grab-and-go cafe. An outdoor terrace hosts a pop-up bar and DJs in summer, residents and locals can join in with events such as candle crafting and collaging, and the theatres and arts venues of the South Bank are right on your doorstep.

*157 Tower Bridge Road, SE1 3LW*
*Nearest station: London Bridge*
*lockeliving.com/en/london/bermonds-locke*

17

# THE MITRE
# HAMPTON COURT

*Tudor hangout turned riverside retreat*

This one-time stopover of Henry VIII's courtiers
has oodles of charm. Creaky floorboards and slop-
ing ceilings give away its age, but everything else
is quirkily designed with bold colour and textures.
Go all out in the Catherine Parr and Henry suites:
each includes sumptuous sofas, luxurious four-
posters and deep copper bathtubs. There are several
spots to eat, drink and be merry here, from the laid-
back Coppernose Bar for breakfast and Sunday
roasts to the 1665 Riverside Brasserie, where diners
can enjoy views over the river while tucking into
British-Italian cuisine. In summer, take afternoon
tea on the terrace, before exploring the gardens at
neighbouring Hampton Court.

*Hampton Court Road, East Molesey, KT8 9BN*
*Nearest station: Hampton Court*
*mitrehamptoncourt.com*

18

# THE TWENTY TWO

*Classical French style with a contemporary twist*

The Portland stone facade could be mistaken for an elegant private residence, and that's exactly how you are welcomed the moment you enter. Parisian flair is evident in the boudoir-style bedrooms, with sumptuous fabrics, heavy curtains, and bathrooms in chequered black and white marble, and all rooms have four-posters and freestanding tubs. You'll find minibars stocked with treats (both naughty and nice), huge flat screen TVs, and pouches stuffed with toiletries in case you left something at home. The blue-panelled restaurant offers British dishes with a Mediterranean twist, but the hotel's best-kept secret is the subterranean nightspot: follow the leopard print carpet downstairs and join the party on the dancefloor.

*22 Grosvenor Square, W1K 6LF*
*Nearest station: Marble Arch*
*the22.london*

19

# THE LONDON EDITION

*Luxurious refuge with fantastic food*

After shopping on Oxford Street and sightseeing in town, this is the perfect place to retreat and refuel. Sink into soft leather sofas in the marble lobby, or try your hand at snooker beneath a giant silver orb suspended from the ornate ceiling. Flagship restaurant Berners Tavern, helmed by chef Jason Atherton, is a favourite of those in the know. Dine on elevated British fare while gazing at the paintings that cover every inch of the restaurant walls, before winding down with cocktails in Punch Room. Bedrooms are more pared-back but still luxurious with wood-panelled walls and shaggy comforters, and (if you're lucky enough to have the spare cash) the views over Fitzrovia from the suites are incredible. No matter which room you choose, you will wake up feeling wonderfully lucky to be in such an oasis of calm in central London.

*10 Berners Street, W1T 3NP*
*Nearest stations: Tottenham Court Road, Oxford Circus*
*editionhotels.com/london*

20

# CLARIDGE'S

*Majestic Mayfair mainstay*

From hosting royalty to being all the rage in the Roaring Twenties, Claridge's remains one of London's most iconic hotels. The grand lobby is a place to see and be seen, and offers a multitude of chic eating and drinking spots. Enjoy the famous afternoon tea accompanied by tinkling piano in the Foyer, or settle in at one of the hotel's bars: the moody Fumoir is all art deco lacquer and crystal, while the intimate pink marble Painter's Room oozes timeless glamour. For coffee and pastries, Claridge's ArtSpace is in an adjoining mews, where you can also peruse exhibitions. The bedrooms are as luxurious as you'd expect, configured by a host of lauded designers, and include opulent suites and sleekly modern rooms.

*Brook Street, W1K 4HR*
*Nearest station: Bond Street*
*claridges.co.uk*

21

# CHILTERN FIREHOUSE

*One of the hottest hotels in town*

This Victorian red-brick fire station, reimagined as a glamorous hotel and restaurant, has been a firm favourite of A-listers and the fashion crowd since it opened its doors a decade ago. The decor is pure art deco decadence, and The Firehouse restaurant is a much coveted dinner destination. Plenty of peacocking goes on here, so sink into a velvet booth and indulge in a side of celeb spotting to go with your truffle scrambled eggs and crab beignets. In the more discreet Ladder Shed bar (open to hotel guests only), sip Perrier-Jouët among the palms and wait for the evening to descend into a DJ-fuelled dance party, knowing you don't have far to roll to bed. The lavish bedrooms feature mahogany headboards and baroque printed carpets, with equally luxurious bathrooms.

*1 Chiltern Street, W1U 7PA*
*Nearest stations: Baker Street, Bond Street*
*chilternfirehouse.com*

22

# BROWN'S

*History in the heart of Mayfair*

It's no surprise that London's oldest hotel is in one of the city's most exclusive postcodes, just a short stroll from Bond Street, the home of luxury shopping. Within the warren of wood-panelled rooms you'll find crackling fires, plush armchairs, elaborate floral wallpapers and mirror-polished surfaces. For the ultimate luxury, check in to the newly minted Sir Paul Smith suite, which features hand-selected pieces of furniture and an eclectic collection of artworks curated by the legendary British designer. Follow in Queen Victoria's footsteps and take afternoon tea in the genteel Drawing Room, or head to all-day bar and restaurant Charlie's for classic British fare and desserts served with theatrical flair from a silver trolley.

*33 Albemarle Street, W1S 4BP*
*Nearest station: Piccadilly Circus*
*roccofortehotels.com/hotels-and-resorts/-s-hotel*

23

# CHARLOTTE STREET HOTEL

*Fitzrovia favourite with a luxury cinema*

Behind the subtle mint green facade of Charlotte Street Hotel is an elegant yet bold interior featuring creative director and founder Kit Kemp's designs throughout. In the brightly muralled Oscar Bar & Restaurant you can enjoy tempting modern European cuisine, and take afternoon tea with a twist (or a white chocolate pistachio cocktail) while lounging on pink and blue pouffes. Bedrooms are a joyful riot of pattern and print with statement headboards, and some suites have separate drawing rooms. You're within easy walking distance of Oxford Circus, Soho and Covent Garden here, but if you'd rather hide away in the enchanting library or book a screening in the private cinema, we certainly won't blame you.

*15–17 Charlotte Street, WIT IRJ*
*Nearest station: Goodge Street, Tottenham Court Road*
*firmdalehotels.com/hotels/london/charlotte-street-hotel*

24

# THE CONNAUGHT

*Pleasure-seeker's paradise*

At this Mayfair institution you will be thoroughly spoiled. Gourmands can make a beeline for the three Michelin-starred Hélène Darrozze restaurant (with specially commissioned Damien Hirst artworks), enjoy elevated dining at Jean-Georges, or sink into a booth at the chilled Colony Grill. Guests can pass through a velvet-curtained doorway into chic hideaway the Red Room, or have a nightcap at the award-winning Connaught Bar. It's clear those who stay here enjoy the finer things, from a Cohiba in the dedicated cigar room to treatments at the Aman Spa, which features a water wall cascading into the pool. The bespoke bedrooms are super-deluxe, and each guest is personally attended by a private butler. If your paycheck, like ours, doesn't stretch that far, a trip to the Connaught patisserie is still not to be missed.

*6 Carlos Place, W1K 2AL*
*Nearest station: Bond Street*
*the-connaught.co.uk*

25

# KETTNER'S TOWNHOUSE

*Decadent Soho hangout*

Once home to London's first ever French restaurant, and frequented by Oscar Wilde, Winston Churchill and Agatha Christie, Kettner's Townhouse has seen its fair share of scandal including a royal affair or two. While it may have shaken its risqué reputation, the hotel is no less splendid today. Dine on British food with a Mediterranean twist in the Clarence Tavern restaurant, before settling into the glamorous Champagne Bar – which is perfect for carousing into the small hours. Bedrooms pay homage to the glitzy decadence of the Roaring Twenties, with scalloped velvet headboards, floral wallpapers, and chintzy sofas, and several have freestanding baths.

*29 Romilly Street, W1D 5HP*
*Nearest station: Leicester Square*
*sohohouse.com/restaurants/kettners-soho*

26

# HAM YARD HOTEL

*Arty hideout with a bowling alley and cinema*

Just minutes from bustling Piccadilly Circus, in a discreet Soho courtyard, is Ham Yard Hotel. The interior is filled with colour and print, comfy sofas and eclectic artworks, and characterful rooms are individually designed. The all-day bar and restaurant is a great place to linger over lunch, or visit the Orangery to indulge in the hotel's renowned afternoon tea. If you prefer to hide away from other guests, head to the snug Library, or up to the leafy roof terrace, which is also home to two lovingly tended beehives. You might be right on Soho's doorstep – with all its theatre, restaurants and nightlife – but you'll also find plenty here to keep you occupied: there's a tranquil spa along with a bowling alley and private cinema downstairs.

*1 Ham Yard, W1D 7DT*
*Nearest station: Piccadilly Circus*
*firmdalehotels.com/hotels/london/ham-yard-hotel*

27

# ARTIST RESIDENCE

*Pimped-out Pimlico townhouse*

This handsome townhouse with candy-striped awnings brings the brand's signature quirky style to an otherwise sedate neighbourhood. Undone charm creeps into every corner: exposed brick, an eclectic mash-up of upcycled furniture, original wooden flooring, neon signage and bold artworks. Roberts radios, mini bars full of artisan treats, and Bramley bath products are standard in the hotel's ten bedrooms, but for the ultimate sleepover book the Grand Suite, where you can sink into a wrought-iron four-poster. The all-day restaurant, which attracts locals and residents alike, offers wholesome fare, and you can enjoy a nightcap in the speakeasy-style basement bar. Breakfast on a stack of exceptional pancakes before heading out to explore the area – you're just a short hop from Tate Britain, Chelsea and Westminster.

*52 Cambridge Street, Pimlico, SW1V 4QQ*
*Nearest stations: Victoria, Pimlico*
*artistresidence.co.uk/london*

28

# THE PRINCE AKATOKI

*Japanese zen in central London*

This hushed sanctuary feels worlds away from nearby bustling Oxford Street. Akatoki means 'new dawn' in Japanese, and you'll begin to rejuvenate as soon as you step inside. The rising sun motif is a reminder of new beginnings that is repeated throughout the soothing bedrooms, which include Malin + Goetz toiletries and yukata robes. Hide away in the moody Malt Lounge, an elegant tearoom that evolves into a whisky bar come evening, where Japanese poetry is etched onto the panelled walls and guests can buy their favourite whisky from the private cabinet and store it there for their next visit. For high-end Japanese cuisine, slide into a booth at TOKii restaurant or grab a seat at the chef's counter (made from molten lava rock) for a sushi masterclass.

*50 Great Cumberland Place, W1H 7FD*
*Nearest station: Marble Arch*
*theprinceakatokilondon.com*

29

# THE PRINCESS ROYAL, NOTTING HILL

*Regal pub restaurant with rooms*

Striding along Westbourne Grove you might think the forest-green facade of The Princess Royal houses just another pub, but it's a gem you'll wish you had discovered sooner. A favourite gathering spot for locals, you'll find a light-filled conservatory with striped banquettes, a marble-topped bar and olive trees. Feast on British-Mediterranean plates from acclaimed chef Ben Tish (try whipped nduja and fennel biscuits) or sample seasonal oysters and razor clams from the raw bar. If you've eaten yourself into a food coma, simply retreat to one of the four funky bedrooms. Next morning one of the best fry-ups in town will set you up for exploring Notting Hill's vintage boutiques.

*47 Hereford Road, W2 5AH*
*Nearest station: Royal Oak, Bayswater*
*cubitthouse.co.uk/the-princess-royal-notting-hill*

30

# THE CADOGAN, A BELMOND HOTEL

*Aristocratic Chelsea townhouse*

Global hotelier Belmond are best known for lavish properties that ooze showy, five-star luxury, yet their London outpost is this quietly elegant residence in Chelsea. The experience is no less luxe, though. On arrival you'll be whisked upstairs by uniformed staff and sequestered in one of their spacious rooms, where sumptuous furnishings in subdued tones and bold artworks sit against period panelling, and marble bathrooms have views over the illustrious neighbourhood. Classic European dishes are served from breakfast through to dinner at The LaLee, inspired by Lillie Langtry, the glamorous socialite who used to reside here, while an indulgent afternoon tea at Maison Lounge is one of the best you'll find in Chelsea.

*75 Sloane Street, SW1X 9SG*
*Nearest stations: Knightsbridge, Sloane Square*
*belmond.com/hotels/europe/uk/london/*
*belmond-cadogan-hotel*

# 31
# NOBU LONDON PORTMAN SQUARE

*Japanese elegance with a world-class restaurant*

This hotel is a lesson in minimalist luxury from the moment you step inside the airy double-height lobby, all floor-to-ceiling glass and curved sofas. Stylish simplicity is carried throughout the bedrooms, with their clean lines and muted tones, and breakfast in bed is delivered to you in a chic bento box. Dining at the restaurant is a must, and don't be surprised if you spot a celebrity or two sampling the signature black cod. Enjoy a cocktail inspired by the founder's travels at the Nobu Bar, and a Japanese-inspired afternoon tea at the Lounge. You can work it all off at the 24-hour gym (complete with Pilates studio), or sink further into your zen with a massage at the Wellness Centre.

*22 Portman Square, W1H 7BG*
*Nearest stations: Marble Arch, Bond Street*
*london-portman.nobuhotels.com*

32

# INHABIT
# QUEEN'S GARDENS

*Restful retreat with a focus on wellness*

Situated on a quiet square in Bayswater, this elegant townhouse provides a peaceful sanctuary not far from Paddington. The relaxed Scandi-style lobby features a curated library of inspirational reads and nature-inspired artworks by local artists. The airy bedrooms are a study in tranquillity (you can choose an in-room scent to suit your mood), and feature muted furnishings and walls painted in a serene palette. You're encouraged to partake in a gadget detox during your stay, and can indulge in treatments at the underground spa or sweat it out at the compact gym and yoga studio. After steaming off in the infrared sauna, head to the Yeotown cafe, where vegan-friendly dishes are served all day.

*1–2 Queen's Gardens, w2 3ba*
*Nearest station: Paddington*
*queensgardens.inhabithotels.com*

33

# BEAVERBROOK TOWN HOUSE

*Thespian-inspired luxury in Sloane country*

A stone's throw from Sloane Square and the buzzy King's Road is the chic sister hotel to luxurious country pad Beaverbrook. From the moment you click your heels across the black and white chequered floor, you are certain to be well looked after. Each of the 14 rooms and suites nod to the city's vibrant theatre scene, and you'll find bespoke four-poster beds with sumptuous fabrics alongside complimentary minibars that you're encouraged to raid, luxurious bath products, and TVs that pop out from the end of your bed. The hotel's Japanese restaurant and bar The Fuji Grill serves a delicious omakase menu and cocktails in an elegant pistachio-panelled room.

*115–116 Sloane Street, SW1X 9PJ*
*Nearest station: Sloane Square*
*beaverbrooktownhouse.co.uk*

34

# THE BERKELEY

*The belle of Belgravia*

Staying at the Berkeley is the ultimate indulgence. This is luxury at its finest, and you'll be welcomed with exquisite homemade pastries and personalised bathrobes with your initials on upon arrival. Each bedroom is entirely unique, but common themes include sweeping curved sofas and dramatic fireplaces, while individual touches range from huge cinema screens to wraparound terraces with views over Belgravia. You could easily spend days here hopping between the in-house restaurants and bars, from Michelin-starred Marcus to the art deco Blue Bar. The sleek Cédric Grolet patisserie commands a queue every day, and the hotel's Prêt-à-Portea afternoon tea is the stuff of legend. For more pampering, head to the Bamford Wellness Spa before lounging by the rooftop pool.

*Wilton Place, SW1X 7RL*
*Nearest station: Hyde Park Corner*
*the-berkeley.co.uk*

35

# THE LOST POET

*Quirky haven in the heart of Notting Hill*

Hundreds of tourists wander past The Lost Poet every day, unaware of the hotel hidden among the pretty pastel townhouses. Behind its doors is a private guesthouse that's home to four individually designed bedrooms, offering peaceful seclusion in notoriously busy Notting Hill. Both the name of the hotel and its decor reference the area's romantic and artistic heritage, and individual colour schemes in each room are inspired by the rainbow facades of Portobello Road. Quirky furnishings include antiques from the famous market and reclaimed school desks fashioned into shelves, and the largest suite boasts a private rooftop terrace. There's no restaurant here, but delicious Ottolenghi breakfast pastries and fresh orange juice are delivered to your door every morning.

*6 Portobello Road, W11 3DG*
*Nearest station: Notting Hill Gate*
*thelostpoet.co.uk*

36

# BINGHAM RIVERHOUSE

*Former literary haunt by the river*

On a peaceful turn of the Thames, this grand Georgian house was once home to poets Edith Cooper and Katherine Bradley (rooms are named after the Sapphic poems they penned each other), and luminaries such as W.B. Yeats and John Ruskin visited. Now a members' club with a restaurant and rooms that are open to non-members, the playful interior features velvet pouffes under sky-high pastel pink ceilings. Original Penguin editions line the library walls, where tables from the restaurant (helmed by MasterChef winner Steven Edwards) spill over and you can dine on beautifully plated seasonal fare. Overnight guests are encouraged to take breakfast in bed before joining a yoga class in the garden.

*61–63 Petersham Road, TW10 6UW*
*Nearest station: Richmond*
*binghamriverhouse.com*

37

# ROOM2, CHISWICK

*Sustainable serviced apartments*

Proudly branding itself as a 'hometel', Room2 combines all the perks of a hotel with somewhere you'd want to stay a little longer. Occupying a former wallpaper manufacturers, the interiors pay homage to the area's Arts & Craft movement, and you'll find hand-painted coffee tables and wallpapers designed by local artists. Each room has its own kitchen and features fun colour schemes and terrazzo sinks, along with thoughtful touches like a 'bits and bobs' box in case you left your sewing kit or playing cards at home. Sustainability is in the hotel's DNA, from the building's construction through to the e-bikes and vegan toiletries, rooftop beehives producing the honey served at breakfast, and the co-working-space-come-cafe where locals gather for crafty workshops.

*10 Windmill Road, Chiswick, W4 1SD*
*Nearest station: Turnham Green*
*room2.com/chiswick*

38

# THE HOXTON, SHEPHERD'S BUSH

*New kid on the block*

Just a stone's throw from leafy Holland Park, The Hoxton's newest offering continues its urban-cool signature style, with plush velvet sofas dotted around the spacious lobby and a wraparound bar with pink leather stools. In the compact but cosy bedrooms you'll find statement headboards and playful touches such as wiggly mirrors and rattan lampshades. Restaurant Chet's offers tingly Thai-fusion dishes served in an American-style diner (not a combination you'd immediately think of, but trust us, it works!). Bag one of the booths under neon signage and mop up fresh and fiery curries with flaky roti before cooling down with one of Chet's signature milkshakes.

*65 Shepherd's Bush Garden, W12 8QE*
*Nearest station: Shepherd's Bush Market*
*thehoxton.com/london/shepherds-bush*

39

# THE LASLETT

*Relaxed charm with character*

Made famous by a certain rom com, Notting Hill draws a flock of tourists every day, eager to sample its food, nightlife and markets, so finding a peaceful hideaway here is like striking gold. On a quiet side road seek out the row of whitewashed townhouses that have been converted into an elegant hotel. The design pays homage to the area, with vintage cabinets sourced from nearby Portobello Road, and relaxed bedrooms featuring gallery walls showcasing local artists. You can graze from breakfast to dinner at The Henderson Bar & Kitchen, enjoy live music and Sunday brunch under stripy canopies on the outdoor terrace, and in the evening the library becomes a buzzy bar and plays host to oyster parties and taco nights.

*8 Pembridge Gardens, w2 4du*
*Nearest station: Notting Hill Gate*
*living-rooms.co.uk/the-laslett*

40

# THE HARI

*A haven of quiet opulence*

The Hari is a testament to understated luxury, its slick glass facade recognisable only to those in the know. In the bronze two-storey lobby you'll find inviting sofas, stylish bookcases and suited gents sipping cocktails at the bar, and there's an abundance of art on the walls as the hotel champions young artists and displays many pieces from the owners' private collection. Upstairs, rooms are sophisticated with jewel-like pops of colour, and most suites have velvet window seats and private balconies with sweeping views over Hyde Park. The Hari is committed to sustainability and includes fair trade gifts in the rooms, eco-friendly amenities, and bikes for getting around town. The hotel restaurant, Il Pampero, serves exceptional Italian cuisine and is a firm favourite among locals.

*20 Chesham Place, SW1X 8HQ*
*Nearest stations: Sloane Street, Knightsbridge*
*thehari.com*

# IMAGE CREDITS

# CONTRIBUTORS

Gina Jackson is a travel writer and photographer who shares personal recommendations and honest hotel critiques on her Instagram @ginagoesto, as well as writing for *Conde Nast Traveller* and Mr & Mrs Smith. While often found in far-flung destinations and testing hotel rooms across the country (Gina also authored *British Boutique Hotels* by Hoxton Mini Press), she is a proud Londoner and loves finding hidden gems across her home city.

Hoxton Mini Press is a small indie publisher based in east London. We make books about London (and beyond) with a dedication to lovely, sustainable production and brilliant photography. When we started the company, people told us 'print was dead'; we wanted to prove them wrong. Books are no longer about information but objects in their own right: things to collect and own and inspire. We are an environmentally conscious publisher, committed to offsetting our carbon footprint. This book, for instance, is 100 per cent carbon compensated, with offset purchased from Stand for Trees.

# INDEX

*An Opinionated Guide to London Hotels*
First edition

Published in 2023 by Hoxton Mini Press, London
Copyright © Hoxton Mini Press 2023. All rights reserved.

Text by Gina Jackson
Copy-editing by Gaynor Sermon
Proofreading by Octavia Stocker
Design by Richard Mason
Production by Sarah-Louise Deazley
Production and editorial support by Georgia Williams

With thanks to Matthew Young for initial series design.

Please note: we recommend checking the websites listed for each
entry before you visit for the latest information on price, opening times
and pre-booking requirements.

A CIP catalogue record for this book is available from the British Library.

ISBN: 978-1-914314-36-0

Printed and bound by OZGraf, Poland

Hoxton Mini Press is an environmentally conscious publisher, committed
to offsetting our carbon footprint. This book is 100 per cent carbon
compensated, with offset purchased from Stand For Trees.

For every book you buy from our website, we plant a tree:
www.hoxtonminipress.com

FSC
www.fsc.org

MIX
Paper from
responsible sources
FSC® C163799